D0147693

TRANSITIONS

Jessica Kingsley Publishers will donate at least
5p per book sold to Gendered Intelligence
(registered charity no. 1182558)

of related interest

Trans Love
An Anthology of Transgender and Non-Binary Voices
Edited by Freiya Benson
ISBN 978 1 78592 432 3
eISBN 978 1 78450 804 3

Trans Power
Own Your Gender
Juno Roche
ISBN 978 1 78775 019 7
eISBN 978 1 78775 020 3

Life Isn't Binary
On Being Both, Beyond, and In-Between
Meg-John Barker and Alex Iantaffi
Foreword by CN Lester
ISBN 978 1 78592 479 8
eISBN 978 1 78450 864 7

Queer Sex
A Trans and Non-Binary Guide to Intimacy,
Pleasure and Relationships
Juno Roche
ISBN 978 1 78592 406 4
eISBN 978 1 78450 770 1

Transitions

Our Stories of Being Trans

Den Casey, Kole Fulmine, Danielle Hopkins,
Kirrin Medcalf, Harry Mizumoto, Tash Oakes-Monger,
Edward Whelan and Ezra Woodger

Foreword by Sabah Choudrey, Juno Roche and Meg-John Barker
Afterword by Dr Jay Stewart, CEO, Gendered Intelligence

Jessica Kingsley Publishers
London and Philadelphia

First published in Great Britain in 2021
by Jessica Kingsley Publishers
An Hachette Company

1

A CIP catalogue record for this title is available from the
British Library and the Library of Congress

ISBN 978 1 78775 851 3
eISBN 978 1 78775 852 0

Printed and bound in Great Britain by TJ Books Limited

Jessica Kingsley Publishers' policy is to use papers that
are natural, renewable and recyclable products and made
from wood grown in sustainable forests. The logging and
manufacturing processes are expected to conform to the
environmental regulations of the country of origin.

Jessica Kingsley Publishers
Carmelite House
50 Victoria Embankment
London EC4Y 0DZ

www.jkp.com

Contents

Foreword

*Sabah Choudrey, Juno Roche
and Meg-John Barker*

The three of us – Sabah Choudrey, Juno Roche and Meg-John Barker (along with Yvy De Luca) – formed the judging panel for the inaugural JKP Writing Prize. The prize was for trans and/or non-binary writers, and contributors were invited to submit original, own-voice stories on the theme of 'trans everyday'. Here we introduce the collection by discussing why we think a book like this is so vital, what stood out for us about the contributions, and where we'd like to see the future of trans writing going.

Why is a collection like this important?
Sabah: We, as trans, non-binary and gender fluid people, know that our stories are often portrayed as

negative, painful or heart-breaking. That might be what we carry every day but it isn't our lives every day. We are more than that. This collection is exactly what I want to see. It reminds us that we are more, we are exceptional, and we are a little bit special. We are ordinary, average, and sometimes quite clumsy. This collection is ours.

Juno: A collection like this is important as it shows trans writing breaking out of the binary – I was in A and then I moved to B, or us explaining ourselves to them for the benefit of them, space. The writing in this collection feels fresh, exciting and most importantly spacious.

Meg-John: For me it's three key reasons – perhaps to summarize some of what others have already brought up here. First, this kind of collection is vital as we live through this ever-continuing moral panic about trans people. We need to write our lives out loud in a world where we're demonized, pathologized, and our very existence is denied, as an act of resistance and survival. Second, in a world where the stories that get told about trans people are so limited, and trans people are so objectified – as highlighted in the recent Disclosure documentary[1] – we really need to get alternative stories of trans lives out there. Collections like this, and *Non-Binary Lives*,[2] do a great job of demonstrating how diverse trans people are, how our lives don't only revolve around our transness, and how our genders intersect with other aspects of our experience. Finally, I think it's powerful for us, as trans people, to have the opportunity to write our stories and have them celebrated, and it's powerful for trans and non-binary folks to read such stories and see their own experiences mirrored. There's an important sense of belonging that comes from being included in a collection like this, and from reading a collection like this.

What themes/stories stand out to you personally?

Juno: What stands out for me are the ideas around our bodies and our lives as being nuanced and connected to gender and the wider structures of gender rather than the simple process of becoming. The stories

---

1   Sam Feder and Amy Scholder, 2020. More details at: www.disclosurethemovie.com

2   Edited by Jos Twist, Ben Vincent, Meg-John Barker and Kat Gupta, Jessica Kingsley Publishers. London, 2020.

speak to gender in its widest context and therefore bring forwards a universality to the content.

Meg-John: I think for me what stand out are the beautiful small moments of everyday life that people capture: both the moments of mutual recognition and connection with other trans folk, and the moments of solitude and connection with our surroundings. I'm thinking, for example, of the vignettes Tash shares of a day trip to Brighton with friends, surviving family Christmases via group chat, crying together after the election. Or Ezra's story of finding kinship with a trans kid over his jacket. Or the importance of Kirrin's LGBTQ mutual aid group during the pandemic. And I'm also thinking of Kirrin's solo journey through East London's green spaces, picking wild garlic; of Edward taking the long route to work so he can look down at the river from the bridge to soothe his anxious inner child; and of Harry eating the banana in the kitchen as the rain falls outside. These moments of connection with others and place seem to be the important ones in which we're affirmed in our experience, and simultaneously liberated from being trapped in outside views of us and our transness.

Sabah: I agree with Meg-John, it's the small moments captured by these incredible writers in the writing that stand out for me, in particular the pauses and dead time where nothing is seemingly happening, just that we are existing. We don't have to explain ourselves all the time. We can just take a moment, no need to say why, and just be.

What is the future of trans writing?

Meg-John: Personally I'm fascinated by the emergence of so many amazing trans creatives during this time of trans moral panic. It's deeply sad that we're going through a time when even the pandemic doesn't seem to halt regular stigmatizing headlines and ill-informed celebrities engaging in 'trans debate'. And it's horrendous that those who do create into this rotten culture are subject to so much attack. But it is wonderful indeed that we've got to the point where it would take far too long to list all the powerful trans writers and other creatives who are out there, just in the UK. As I said in my blog post for JKP in the run up to the prize, I love the fact that trans creatives like Travis Alabanza, CN Lester, Amrou Al-Kadhi and Juliet Jacques – and you two of course! – are troubling conventional trans narratives in their memoirs, and putting out all kinds of stories about transness, centring different intersections, and querying binaries such as pride and shame, pre and post, man and woman, cis and trans, euphoria and dysphoria, and more.

Sabah: That's it – more voices, more explorations and more questions. As humans we are expert at asking, 'why?' As trans people we are expert at asking, 'why not?' We can write our own futures because the future of trans writing is truly ours. The proof is right here in your hands.

Juno: The future is endless. We have only just started.

We Are Everywhere

Tash Oakes-Monger

Sitting down to write this, there are lots of trans everyday stories I could tell. The story of patience while waiting for gender clinics, for surgeries, for hormones, for acceptance. The story of shame and sadness, of coming out, of being in the closet, of parents and work and doctors. The particular story of my body and scars and pain and change and healing. There is a narrative that is expected, one that is medicalized and pathologized and sad and alone. But this is my chance to tell a story, and the one I want remembering is one of queer rage and joy and untouchable love between trans people.

It is Christmas and we are all separated to our family homes. Before we part, we set up an emoji code for our group chat. Symbols for when we are misgendered, when we are sad, when we need an emergency call. We keep in contact, sending voice notes and videos, photos and words of encouragement. When it is over, we return to London and congregate at Freddy's. We make pancakes in the kitchen and dance to old songs. We spill out the pain of the week that has been. It is a catharsis. We get into bed and pass a smoke around. We nap, and when we wake up, everything feels better.

One weekend in February we get the train to Brighton, and Toby is wearing a fur coat that he found for £15. It is white and soft and like something from a fashion show, and he is delighted. I am wearing dungarees and Freddy has a dangling skeleton earring in his right ear. We get a lot of looks; it isn't a surprise. We dance down the platform, singing and laughing. We share a double bed for the weekend. We buy the biggest jar of jalapeños and bend double with the hilarity of it. We share a bath. Our bodies normally bound and covered, but not now. The gentleness of this moment, the vulnerability to see them like this, is the biggest privilege of my life. Freddy does a face mask and we are near crying with laughter when it won't come off. We cook up a feast and do tarot readings at the table. We watch a movie with popcorn and talk into the night. We triple spoon.

The morning brings coffee and seagulls and walks around junk stores. We do one of those photo booths and capture the bliss of it all in black and white. We lie on the beach and hold hands and let the wind rush around us. We run in the sea and Freddy mistimes a wave jump and gets soaked. We get tattoos, inking the words we know to be true: *Our queer love cannot be taken, our queer joy cannot be taken.*

I fall in love with another trans person, and they touch my scars like they are nothing and everything at the same time. They look at me and they see me, and it is the greatest gift of them all. When they are sad, I pull their feet on to mine and dance us around the living room. They wear my jumpers and I can almost feel the warmth in them from across the room. We clean our teeth holding hands, and escaping tooth-paste always stains something. They bring me tea in bed, and we are always drawing each other closer.

The sun goes down in Brighton and we eat fish and chips in a tiny shop. Toby orders gravy on his and licks it from his fingers. We are talking about all the laws that stop us from living our lives. We are talking about marriage and adoption and love and names, and then suddenly Toby is howling at photos of a time I tried to grow out my hair. We can't stop laughing then at his face. My heart is swollen with it all.

The ticket inspector lets us off when a railcard is forgotten on the way home. I make a video on my phone of the weekend while the others snooze. I am almost shocked by the utter happiness in the clips. I was not told that trans people were allowed such things.

On a Friday night we gather in a swimming pool in Lewisham; they close the pool so that only trans people can use the session and we can swim in peace. In the changing rooms we take off our day wear. I see someone in a business suit pull down the drab grey to reveal a pink dress underneath. I smile at them, they smile back. In the water we can be just us. Our bodies and our swimming wear accepted. Ariel carries Freddy like a baby in their arms. They sing a song together as they walk through the water. Toby gives me a piggyback and we fall into the water laughing. We share out shampoo when we go to shower.

Xan is crocheting a blanket in the colours of the trans flag. They meet Toby for the first time and a week later offer the blanket to him when it is finished. We attend a trans yoga class and Toby laughs through the poses. Xan puts their arms around Freddy and he lies in my lap. We go for pizza after and talk about the smallest and the biggest things you can imagine.

Me and Freddy sit and go through their bank statements and I call the phone company to get them a cheaper bill. We write poems in a closing Pret with hot chocolate, and when they kick us out, Freddy asks to take the pastries they are going to throw away. We eat almond croissants in the street. There are boxes of Toby's things in my flat, parts of my friends littered in my life. When money is tight, we transfer enough to get by, we take on more of the coffee orders, we are each other's insurance systems.

The night of the general election, when I arrive home after a day of knocking doors and talking to voters, when my feet are aching and face chapped with wind, when the exit poll comes out and my heart breaks clean in two, they arrive. I don't even ask; they just turn up, knock on the door and take me to my room. We take it in turns to cry into each other with the fear and devastation and rage of such an important loss. The three of us eat oven chips out of a Pyrex dish and the saltiness is a balm to our tears. We squeeze into the tiniest bed and hold each other. When the morning comes, we sing Billy Bragg songs at the top of our voices and cook up a breakfast of kings. The sun is shining and something in the togetherness sticks a splinter of hope into the day.

I meet Lu on a retreat and in one weekend they become family. We write to each other for weeks after, about our days, our lives, our worries. They send me postcards and letters and love. In their handwriting is a reverence of our lives that I feel in my gut.

I was out walking last week, and I called Max to catch up. We laugh down the phone as the rain comes down. They know exactly what to say when my ex crops up in my life uninvited. I know if I ever needed anything, they would have my back. They send me photos of the ocean, simply because they know it brings me joy.

Oftentimes my transness leaves me vulnerable to the world. In medical appointments where I am misgendered and my body is talked about in a way that doesn't belong to me. In the street when I am spat on. On the Tube several times a week when people debate my gender right in front of me. In changing rooms when I am asked to leave. But each and every time I pick up my phone and message my trans loved ones, they are there. A beacon of power and of changing the way things are. They challenge me to love bigger and better and bolder. We plan a family where we can bring up kids who know that their gender is theirs to decide and experience and find joy in. Trans people taught me this.

There is a bit in the movie *Pride* where Joe, a young gay man, has been outed to his family. His mum sits him down for a talk on his bed in his tiny bedroom, and this scene embodies something that I've only really understood recently. She sits next to him crying and says, 'It's such a terrible life, Joe. It's lonely. Is that what you want? No family. Hiding from people at work. From everyone. Keeping secrets.' By this point in the film you've watched his family tiptoe around one another with a level of formality and decorum that bleeds all joy and love from their lives. The whole thing reeks of keeping up appearances. Meanwhile, Joe is marching on the streets, making banners in bookshops, sharing his first kiss on the dance floor, and travelling across the country in a theatre van to stand with those on the picket line. His life is bursting with vibrancy and love and solidarity and joy. It reminds me of my own life. How often I am told that being trans is a terrible life of pain and suffering. And how I am able to see the whole picture, the camera panning back, the truth.

Today we are 21 days into a national lockdown; everyone fears for the future in this virus apocalypse. And today I know what trans everyday is. It is to be afraid and yet brave; it is to be isolated and yet build community; it is to be separate and yet never alone. It is to create a family and greet them every day with virtual good mornings and tarot readings and photos of baking. It is watching films together and sending each other grow-your-own herb gardens. It is packages that say, 'I love you' and 'I know this is hard but I'm thinking of you'. It is asking for art submissions to create an exhibition in our flat. It is the most beautiful works turning up in the post and now filling the walls. It is reinvesting. It is bold and brilliant and everything I am proud of. The word 'trans' means across or beyond. I think we are beyond. Beyond most of the world's understanding; going above and beyond for each other; breaking down structures that humanity will look back on in a hundred years and be ashamed to have ever defended.

We are everywhere and, yes, we are changing the fabric of society, but my god, who told you that was a bad thing?

Bits and Pieces of Myself

Edward Whelan

I have been sleeping better lately. I get by OK on seven hours' sleep. I still wake with a jolt.

First, make coffee.

Add milk.

I have a routine to my days. A system, to manage the ordinary daily upsets that lead to a spiralling panic.

There is always a bite of anxiety as I leave the house. I keep a hand on it, take a deep breath. I'm often late, lingering in the quiet of the house, checking everything one last time, go to the mirror one last time, before being ready to be out in the scary world.

Brush your teeth for the full two minutes.

Switch on the television.

I watch too much TV, I know. I watch it first thing in the morning in bed, on my phone. I watch TV on my lunch break at work. It's an easy tool to reach for, to calm the anxiety. I use the ceaseless burbling noise of television to keep my head busy. The more noise there is in the room, the less I feel my own stirring anxiety.

Drink a glass of water.

I have carried this anxiety with me for as long as I can remember. It is as if I was born with a twin. I grew up, but they stayed two years old, the age they learnt to scream 'No!' to everything and throw a tantrum at the slightest suggestion that they, I don't know, take a bath or leave the house.

I have to take this difficult, fretting, crying child with me everywhere I go, and if they kick off, then everything has to stop while I calm them down so I can get on with my day. Try to buy train tickets and they wail. Need to make a phone call and they hold their breath and refuse to breathe. Many days it is just easier to go back home and put the TV on until they calm down.

Cycle to work, take the long way round.

Stop on the bridge, look at the river.

There was a peculiar kind of timeslip when I

transitioned. At first, newly out as trans with a shaved head and a binder, I was mistaken for a teenage boy. I was actually 23. Appropriate really, to be given a second chance at being a teenager. My adolescence, the first time round, was when I started to shut down, pushing away new emotions and new experiences. I went through the motions of my life, finishing school, going to university, before finally giving up, age 19, and retreating back to my bedroom for six years. It was all too much.

And then transitioning and the chance for a do-over. There I was, restarting the process of adolescence, walking around in a body that was newly awkward and uncomfortable, and trying to figure out who I was and what the hell I was going to do with my life. It was cutely metaphorical, albeit painful. I felt like a 12-year-old but I had a body over twice that age. As my housemates were moving on from their first crappy graduate jobs, and dumping their crappy university boyfriends and girlfriends, I was going backwards. Body and mind out of synch, hanging between two different times.

Check emails, make a to-do list.

My body has grown and shaped itself all on its own. It did its own thing and all I could do was watch from inside. When your body and mind move in separate directions, stress fractures will appear. This is how the body impacts on the mind. How the weight of a body pulling away can damage and tear at your mind.

I grew a bird on my shoulder. A huge screeching bird that shrieks and drives its talons in under my collarbone. The feeling of gender dysphoria is a screaming, shrieking feeling to me, driving deep into my mind, and I'll do anything to escape it.

I tried to escape my body. Drinking all night sort of works. Starving. Starve yourself enough and your body feels light and remote. Binging works, too. If you eat from the moment you wake up until you crawl into your bed, curtains closed, you lose touch with your body. You have to, to cope with what you're doing to it. I used the tools I had to hand.

When I started transitioning, I changed my body. Now, after 15 years of hormones and several surgeries, my previous body feels like an other-worldly thing. There is a kind of strange floating feeling I get from growing up in one body and now being in another. Moments of vertigo when I am aware of every cut and stitch and skin graft I've had. It's the feeling you get at the end of watching *The Sixth Sense*, when you realize during everything you've seen, you were actually seeing something else, and you feel the whole movie again in a few seconds. I step out of a hot shower and I can see the scars running all over my body, standing out in bright pink. This is the body I built to soothe that hysterical bird on my shoulder. They're another character I still take everywhere with me.

My mind today is built from all these different pieces of myself. It is a mind of separate parts growing around each other, shifting to find space for themselves with a nudge of the elbow, like babies in a womb. I still have my anxiety twin round my feet, still have my hysterical bird, though aged now and mostly quiet. I still have the ghost of the girl I was in high school, from my first adolescence. She's still with me, somewhere at the back. There are others, too.

Five thirty, log out.

Pick up pasta on the way home.

Of course, everyone changes as they grow up. This isn't something special to being trans, to find you have changed. All bodies change. So being trans is not, really, all that radical. It seems to me to be a quite ordinary experience.

But the impact of changing still startles me. I have found changes keep occurring that I just didn't expect. With each physical change I made to my body, however tiny, a new part of myself woke up. A tiny bloom of self-confidence. Here I am shushing someone in the cinema. Or signing up for a ballet class with a room full of strangers. Things I would have only done before with a crushing level of doubt and self-criticism, I now breeze through. Transitioning didn't stop when I was 'passing', or when I'd changed all my paperwork, or when I'd had all the surgeries I wanted. I have finished the physical transition, but the process continues in these unexpected corners. I am guessing this is what being whole feels like. Right now it comes and goes, in flashes. Since I rebooted my life at 23, I have just been trying to get all the pieces of myself assembled and hold them in place while the glue dries.

Key in the lock, switch on the hall light.

I have spent so many years pulling away from my body that it is hard to get back inside it now. I have grown accustomed to ignoring it. I thought it was good if it was in pain; it deserved it, stupid thing. Now, I am trying to reconnect to it. I took up running and found in that how to fuse my mind and body in a way that was bearable. At first I ran too much, the old habit of wanting to give myself pain coming back.

It has taken some time to find a balance, to want to take care of this body. I have been angry with it for so long that this new sense of a body being OK is jarring and unfamiliar. I look at my feet – are these my feet? Do they really belong to me? I poke my stomach. Is it OK to be a bit fat? How do I tell? Over-eating and not eating was for years one way I detached myself from my body, punished it for existing, pushed it away. There is still an echo left when I eat of how it felt to hate it so much. Today I have an uneasy relationship with food; eating can so easily catapult me back in time to being that overweight teenage girl again, all these years later.

And now, at 42 years old, I can see clearly the damage that is done from experiencing myself as a series of detached characters. My sense of self is fragmented and I can find myself drifting apart, bits and pieces of myself moving away from each other. It can feel like I'm dissolving into atoms. So I ground myself in little recurring moments of each day. Making coffee, brushing my teeth. These ordinary daily acts are my touchstones, reminding me I am real, I am here.

An Eagle at Sunset

Den Casey

I'm so nervous. My mouth is so dry I feel like I've been eating chalk. Why am I so nervous? I've been okay on my two other visits, when I was explaining to Mauro what I wanted and he was working on designs. He had been so friendly and non-judgemental, and put me at my ease in no time. So I don't know if now this is a fear of pain or of the finality, or just of feeling like a walking cliché. Probably the last, if I'm honest. Who gets their first tattoo at 62, for godssakes? And the design that had seemed so perfect – was it really just embarrassingly corny? I feel like an idiot – that this whole thing should mean so much, and at my age. Never mind the pain, I am frightened of the other customers finding me ridiculous. Could I stand the self-consciousness for the next three hours? Would they just see me – as I was used to people seeing me, in spite of everything – as an old dyke having a mid-life crisis? (Who am I kidding? I'm not young enough for a mid-life crisis!) I feel old and foolish. It would be the easiest thing in the world to walk straight past the studio, forget the whole thing, go home to Michelle via the new vegan deli, call her and tell her I'm picking up her favourite supper – artichoke hearts and roast baby aubergines with miso dressing.

Yes, it would be so easy. Just walk past and forget the whole thing. Go back to safety, to familiarity and to the woman I love. But I can't. Because I know I want that tattoo so badly. I have dreamt of it for months now. And I know that safety is an illusion. Because after a while it would all start up again. The restlessness, the dissatisfaction. The conversations that go round and round, and I know I test her patience even though she tries not to show it. Conversations that lead to nowhere, because they come from a need in me that only I can address. The need – as an older, non-binary lesbian – to be visible.

I can't keep doing this to her, and I can't keep doing it to myself – getting so far and then backing out. And so, almost dizzy from the combination of strong coffee and overthinking, I push down my feelings as I push open the door of the studio and step inside.

Mauro looks up and gives me that familiar toothy grin. 'So, you didn't change your mind, then?' I smile back, feeling instantly reassured by his friendly demeanour. 'No,' I say. 'No, I didn't change my mind.'

*

I'm telling you this story because getting that tattoo was one of the hardest and most important things I've done in my whole life. It was the day I signalled to myself – and to the world – that I was comfortable with being a non-binary lesbian. That I wanted to be *seen* as a non-binary lesbian. It had taken me 62 long years to get to that point.

Why was getting a tattoo so significant? Well, for all of my adult life I had been seen – and seen myself – as a female lesbian. Before that, I would probably best be described as a confused tomboy. Let's just say if I'd known then what I know now, it would have saved not just years but decades of heartache and feeling like I wasn't fitting in. That's why I got the tattoo, and that's why I need to tell you the story behind it.

I was part of a small lesbian community in the

South of England from the early 1980s. I'd had a hard time accepting my sexuality due to my Christian upbringing, and when I met Michelle ten years later, I knew I had found my soulmate. Not only was she the most caring woman I'd ever met, but she was also from a Christian background, and through many long conversations we found a way to come to terms with our experiences, leave the guilt and rejection behind, and feel happy and secure in our love for each other. It was a marvellous feeling. But looking back, I realize that we just replaced one orthodoxy with another. We were part of a local community of lesbians and gay men who were forging new ways of living, and in many ways these were exciting and happy times. And yet...something was never quite right. The lesbian community I was part of was welcoming but quite rigid – like you had to have similar experiences and views in order to fit in. Of course, being female was never questioned. Shortly after Michelle and I got together, I remember hearing about Drag Kings, which were apparently a big new thing on the scene in some of the larger towns and cities. I was fascinated by these stories and eager to find out more, but they seemed a world away from my quiet life and were frowned upon by the feminist lesbians

I knew. Two of our closest friends, Jean and Carole, often told us stories over dinners or country walks of things that were happening in London that Carole knew about through her job, which put her into contact with a lot of lesbians on the London scene. She told us about these Drag King cabarets, where women would perform as male characters, or about workshops where anyone could get dressed up and come out barely recognizable in their new masculine identities. She even told us about these things called 'T parties', where lesbians would take testosterone together and explore their masculinity. There seemed to be quite a sexual side to it, and I think we were all fascinated by this – we all wanted to hear the stories – but there was an unspoken assumption that these goings-on were something we all disapproved of, and the stories would always end with Carole and Jean laughing about it all, and saying why on earth would lesbians want to be like men? Michelle would laugh in agreement too – she has always been very feminine and happy with being a woman. But I remember feeling very uncomfortable, and rather than joining in with their laughter and condemnation, I would just go quiet. Was this because I was scared to admit that I was a little bit too fascinated? Or was it because I felt confused? Perhaps it was a remnant of my Christian upbringing that the idea of injecting testosterone into your body didn't sit right with me, but the other stuff – the experimenting with identity, exploring masculinity – was something that stirred feelings that went all the way back to my teenage years as that confused tomboy.

*

I came out as non-binary in 2015. A 20-year journey. Jean and Carole are long gone, but many of our old friends still remain and have been willing to understand who I am, to continue to include me, and to use my preferred pronouns. What this journey has shown me is that the world isn't just divided along the gender binary, but along others: the intolerant versus the accepting; the hostile versus the welcoming.

Many of the lesbians in our friendship group are confused as to how I could still be a lesbian, but identify as non-binary. I can understand their confusion, but it's not something I should need to explain. I just *am*, just as they just *are*. It is always the marginalized who are required to explain ourselves. The thing is, they always just assumed I was a female lesbian all these years – not just because of how they read my body, but because of the unspoken assumptions, like in those conversations with Jean and Carole: the climate of intolerance of difference that they had barely noticed, but that had kept me silently uncomfortable and confused for so many years.

Things haven't been that easy at work, either. My colleague Imogen – a heterosexual, cisgender woman – is by far my most supportive ally in the office, and she has done a lot to help make my working life more bearable. When I added my preferred 'They/them' pronouns to my email signature, without saying a word Imogen quietly added 'She/her' to hers. I walked across the office and gave her a big hug. For a long time, it was only the two of us who had our preferred pronouns on our emails, but now quite a few colleagues have also added theirs. This is what allyship is all about – taking some of the weight, sharing the load, so that it's not always the trans or non-binary person who has to bear it alone.

The thing about coming out as non-binary in your 60s is that people have very set ideas about you. The main thing in both work and my friendship group is that even after having come out as non-binary, friends and colleagues don't really take on board what this means and still make assumptions that I am female. Again, I guess it's understandable: many things about me still look the same to them. I haven't felt the need to change my name – I have always been Den, never Denise. My name has always felt comfortably gender-neutral (even before I knew the term), and I have always liked it; it feels like me. Similarly, I haven't felt any desire to change my body – I don't need to validate my identity by injecting testosterone, and have never wished to have any kind of surgery. I strongly feel that having certain physical features doesn't alter who I am inside, and in any case one of the benefits of coming out as non-binary after the menopause is that my body has already become naturally quite masculinized.

But all this leaves me with the problem of having to endlessly come out to people, to endlessly explain, and to have to fight over and over again to make myself visible as a non-binary lesbian, when everyone around me seems to want to push me back into a box they feel comfortable with. So this is where the tattoo comes in. I needed something to make my identity real – primarily to myself, but also to others. A visual reminder of who I am, and a signifier to the world that I'm not going back. Something bold and strong, reflecting who I am and where I am, at this stage in my life.

So I lie back as Mauro wipes my chest and applies the transfer exactly where we have agreed – on the left side, just above my heart. I try not to tense too much as I hear the buzz of the tattoo gun. The initial pain makes me start, but after a while I feel myself rising up through it, coming up through layers of pain like rising through the layers of years and decades. The needle cuts through all the uncertainty and confusion, bringing the most wonderful and unexpected sense of clarity. A feeling of absolute calm and peace descends on me, and I am aware only of Mauro's intense concentration as the outline takes shape.

*

'That's it, all done. Want to take a look?'

I take a while to come back into myself and into the room. I get up slowly, my heart swelling in anticipation, and walk over to the mirror. And there it is, on my chest: me, in eagle form, a silhouette flying out, black and low against a blazing sunset. These may be my sunset years, but who I am is stronger, more fearless and more beautiful than I have ever been before.

I am so excited and elated that I can hardly listen to Mauro's aftercare instructions as he sprays the area with disinfectant, applies Vaseline, covers it with cling film and tapes it down. I can't wait to get outside and get home to Michelle.

I check my watch. Just after five thirty. If I hurry, I'll just catch the vegan deli before it closes. I'll call Michelle – tell her I'm picking up her favourite supper. And then I'll get home as fast as I can, pull her close to me and then stand back and let her see. Let her see *it*, and let her see *me*. A proud, strong, 62-year-old non-binary lesbian. An eagle at sunset.

Walk in My Shoes

Kirrin Medcalf

I'm walking down the street, scarf wrapped around my face and dodging between people I pass, trying to keep as much distance between them and me. No, it's not only the spring of 2020; it's 2019, and 2018, and 2017 and…well, you get the picture. Life outside stays much the same, pandemic or no pandemic. It's the reality of existing outside while trans; of existing on the streets as a gender-nonconforming person; of make-up and long hair on a body that is increasingly read as masculine. There are precautions you have to take. Transphobia and femmephobia are as violent to the body as any virus. It's my everyday, my anyday.

But this isn't an account of the streets of tarmac, or of words and fists as equally hard and unforgiving. You've heard that story, I've heard that story, a million times. It's a truth that needs to be spoken, but when it becomes the only truth that's spoken, it becomes its own myth. There's more to me than the violence inflicted upon me by the people and the structures of this world. My core self grows between the cracks, twisting and turning to make it through, but green and wild all the same.

I slip through the brick gates of Finsbury Park and then on to the old railway line: a small strip of green striving to take back its world from the concrete and stone of the line between Alexandra Palace and Finsbury Park. You could easily mistake the greenery as a new wilding, springing up where it had not been before. This is not the truth. Much like the newspaper pages caught in the brambles proclaiming the 'new' existence of trans people threatening the rights of others, or the newest 'first' that we have supposedly done. The wild garlic that grows along the banks here releases its strong aroma as I gather it for nettle and garlic soup. It hints at an older story, its presence one of the last reminders of an ancient woodland that once stood here.

A quick look at the 1856 Ordnance Survey map details a woodland called Holloway Wood surrounded by open land in this spot. This has been all replaced by rows of houses, railway lines and Finsbury Park by the time of the 1945 Ordnance Survey map. Similarly, when I scour the newspaper archives for whispers of my own cultural inheritance, I come across a similar and brief eagle-eye view of what was. A report from 1839 entitled 'Female husband' details a court case brought forward by an angry mother-in-law upon finding out the man her daughter had married in Highgate church was assigned female at birth. Then on to reports of 'men' in petticoats' in 1870 detailing the trial of Park and Boult, who had been living in apartments together as women but had been assigned male at birth. A more recent tale from 1961 is that of Mr Vensettie who, at 21 years old, appeared in court and the newspapers. He was sent to hospital for 'regarding herself a boy'; an aftercare officer at Clerkenwell commented to the papers that the hospital was 'unable to help her'. The medicalization of transness no more or less able to help us then than now. Our history only recorded in accounts of institutional response, while today trans men still sit in prison for being in relationships with women without disclosing their trans status.

I smile at the mention of Clerkenwell in the article, as I trace the paper footsteps of people long since passed. Clerkenwell, where the after-care officer once stood to tell the tale of another through his own lens, is now home to England's only LGBTQIA+ homelessness shelter and one of many community centres. Stories of criminalization and inappropriate healthcare are still shared here, but now with our own voices, sitting on bean bags and a plush pink bed, with a sign proudly proclaiming 'pegging for peace' above our heads. Our history grows as deep as the roots of the old forest that rot beneath my feet, most of the oral tradition gone, leaving the newspaper articles and court papers, like the wild garlic, as just a small whisper of what once was.

I finish picking the garlic and wrap it in newspaper before storing it safely in my rucksack and continuing on with my walk. Today's route is the one I call my graveyard walk – it's one of my favourites. Along the old railway line, before I cut off to Highgate Cemetery, through Hampstead Heath, to the Friends of Hampstead Cemetery, on to Paddington Old Cemetery and ending at Kensal Green Cemetery: the burial site of James Barry.

Dr James Barry was a surgeon who strongly advocated for, often to his personal detriment, the rights of those seen as less than or other. Through his work he improved the living conditions of enslaved people, prisoners, those with leprosy and the mentally ill, and increased women's chances of surviving caesarean sections. Barry was also no stranger to scandal and was often demoted for his attitude. In 1824 he was accused of sodomy in a public libel case; at the time sexual relations between men were illegal. Upon his death, his direct wishes for the treatment of his body were ignored, and he was discovered to have the primary sex characteristics most commonly associated with women.

A conversation about Barry is hard to have without someone, usually a cis person, reminding you in a condescending tone that you can't call him trans as that wasn't a term used until the 20th century, conveniently forgetting that, with their logic, heterosexuals didn't exist until the 19th century. What existed before that in their minds I cannot imagine – perhaps an alleged backwater, deep, wild and remote that people left for more enlightened times like teenagers fleeing their rural upbringing for the big city. Or, as Barry may have called it, a backwood, not a backwater.

The words are different, but what they describe is the same, or close to it. I think of it as a path that runs parallel to mine. Our destinations might not be the same, nor the directions exact, but I sometimes glimpse him through the trees walking on his path alongside mine. The brambles of time are too thick to walk one another's route, yet I know he is there, his shadow slipping through the trees and falling on to my path, as I walk through the woods, intangible but real and there.

Trees in a hollow are trees in a hollow no matter the name, but the difference between a dell, a dingle and a valley can also be as wide as the forested gaps they describe. Words are useful to pass information on to a fellow traveller, perhaps to locate the site of a fallen tree barricading the path or a fruitful patch for foraging. But to hold one description as truer than the other, or as exactly the same, denies the chance to delight in the nuanced differences located in every term. Each is as rooted in the land and time they spring from as are the people that speak them.

On other days I walk the other way along the railway line, through Finsbury Park to New River Path and past the warehouse district. There I was an extra for a music video by Bitch Hunt, a queer trans rock band, for a song about cis men who take up too much space. At this point my route parts either onwards to Springfield Park and Lea Valley beyond, or to cross to Hackney Marshes and the River Lea.

If I head onwards to Lea Valley, I pass through the canal paths where teenage boys once circled me, shouting 'What are you?' until I managed to lose them by turning a corner and scrambling up the embankment to a road. I hurried home quickly that night, and it took me a long time to walk that route again.

My other option is to cross to the Hackney Marshes and the River Lea, where a trans man taught me how to forage for my first wild garlic. The routes from my history are as marked by acts of solidarity and sharing from trans people as they are by acts of aggression from cis counterparts.

The landmark for today's walk is the men's swimming pond, the only single-sex men's space I've ever used beyond changing rooms in clothes shops. While other trans people who have walked a path similar to mine find using men's spaces to be affirming and welcoming, I just feel almost as uncomfortable in them as I do in women's spaces. Since last summer I've stopped using the men's pond; the one dip into a pond in London broke through the quiet surface of my own mind. The world is full of ponds, lakes and little rivers that are perfect for swimming in, so why wait for the ones which have been divided into two categories that I do not fit?

Transness once again shines a spotlight on to structures and rules that seem natural at first, but upon closer inspection have been pruned and trimmed into place – a trellis I have been taught to unconsciously make for myself. Nowadays I swim whenever I get the chance, in places without changing rooms and without lifeguards. For freedom you sacrifice safety: a truth all trans people know.

I've always found freedom in nature, or perhaps just a pause from the overwhelming commotion of the habitat made for and by us, my autism stopping my brain from filtering out the low hum of electronics wherever I go. Regardless of the reason, the story of myself and the thousands of past selves that have brought me to the me I am today are indistinguishable from the landscapes I grew up in. Their rolling highs and rugged lows are nestled within the current version of me that is laying on the stone wall that edges the men's pond staring up at the blue sky.

During my childhood I lived in wide open spaces. Our family moved around after my father, as the RAF transferred him from place to place. When I was born, we lived in the first cottage in a row of cottages surrounded by fields, a pub ending the small line. A settlement had been on the land where the hamlet now still stands as far back as the Domesday Book. Many years later I found out the pub at the end had been a gay bar when I was born, prophetic of the queer culture that would exist present but unknown, and just out of reach until I was an adult. We moved by the time I was four, my sister newly born on the living-room floor, and my father posted across the country within weeks of her birth.

From house to house we moved, all utilitarian squares, all indistinguishable from the hundreds of their pur-pose-built neighbours. What I do remember of them was the world around them: stars from the small win-dow above my bed in a house we stayed in for only three months; at the next it's the pigs that ate my elastic-band-powered airplane in the field backing on to the garden. Then the last RAF house with open fields alongside where I learnt to ride a bike and drew on the side of the house with the natural chalk of Chiltern soil. After the end of the RAF years were two more homes: there was the house with the willow tree I played under, and then the cold white house in the shade of Bacombe Hill.

My favourite memories from childhood are all of the outdoors. Playing Famous Five with my best friend, running between ivy-covered trees next to the canal. I was always George Kirrin, the 'girl' who dressed like a boy, looked like a boy and was angry whenever anyone used 'she' instead of 'him'. Under those dusty canopies of trees my gender began to grow and take form, to the extent that George Kirrin became my gender during my youth, and later Kirrin became my name. I have taken a part of that childhood laughter, freedom and adventure found in those woods and potted it within my name to be carried around in my everyday life.

In the books, George had a dog, Timmy. Of course, this meant that I also had to have a dog, an attempt to answer the yearning within me that I had yet to put a name to, that called for me to be something other than what I was told I was. It became the most important relationship in my life, the bond between my dog, Holly, and me. A bond that kept me alive through my teenage years; like many other autistic and trans people, my closest friend was not of the same species as me.

Wherever I had free time that wasn't spent with Holly, such as lunch break at school, it was spent up a tree with my few human friends. My closest school friend also turned out to be neurodiverse and queer, not that we knew then the names for the strange bonds between us. An English teacher passing by once exclaimed that from the outside we appeared like a talking tree. For that moment we were not hobbits perched upon a living tree, but we were Treebeard himself, wobbling the branches in time with our speech to add to the illusion.

That sense has never quite left me: of being a tree but not a tree, clinging to the branches with those who are like me. The separation between self and the natural world has never happened for me, nor has it lost the comfort it offered to me as a child. When my crush got with someone else, I threw a tent into the back of my rickety first car and drove to Germany to cry in foreign fields. After healing from top surgery, I celebrated by packing my car again and left to go swimming in a river. My gender and self are part of nature, and within them there is comfort and joy; we are the wild things.

The sun is starting to set low, and I move from where I have been lying by the side of the swimming ponds. I don't turn for home just yet as I am not tired, and I always enjoy racing the light to get home at the last minute. The people I pass as I head into the woods are doing the same, trying to wring out any extra seconds of their one walk a day under lockdown, but sticking to the main paths. I am no more afraid of going off path than I am of the future. We queers are good at finding out how to survive in any new situation; we stick together and know how to share. While my local area group struggles to work out what mutual aid and community mean, the LGBTQI mutual aid group is already in full swing, the notifications popping up on my phone to read once home.

We are tethered to the earth by the history of those who have walked unseen before us and by the little acts of solidarity between us now; we are part of it rather than walking upon it. My everyday, my anyday, is tied to a million others' everydays. Like the wild garlic's individual shoots growing so close to one another you cannot see where one plant ends and another begins. Together we grow under dappled light in places that are easily overlooked, our history fighting against fading from cultural memory. But for me it's now time for home, for wild garlic and nettle soup, and to continue growing.

The One That No One Talks About / Alice What's the Matter? (Delete as Appropriate)

Danielle Hopkins

My phone alarm goes off.

'Far from Love' blares loudly from the speaker as the vocals blur and blend into the usual morning ritual. Hopefully, it will bring me to a fully awakened state.

It does not.

Fighting and striving whilst wrapped in a myriad of covers and sheets, I struggle to locate where the noise is coming from. Eventually, my body arrives at its senses, and I am awake enough to stop the beautiful dream-like music from waking the rest of the street, let alone me.

I am tired, real tired. It's Day 'something', post-Gender Reassignment Surgery, and for weeks now the routine has been the same. I wake from the tormented sleep, full of worry, to see if I will awake with blood, pus or something else in my overnight pad.

The recovery from surgery has been fraught with difficulties and everything from a paramedic visit through to suspected kidney stones and a UTI. My body is still trying to fight and fight hard against a deep surgical infection that shows no signs of abating for good. Vanquished. Defeated.

'We' had been close a few times. A few salad days when I'd woken and there was nothing. Usually, I slid my tracksuit bottoms down and then my pants. Then gingerly, not wanting there to be any infection there, my pad. Each day expectant that the pad would be clean. No blood, no pus, just nothing. For a few brief moments the anticipation reached a crescendo of intense thoughts: *Will today be the day I can sigh with relief? Will this be the moment I can get up and get on with my recovery from surgery without having the very real fear that bits would fall out from where they really, really should not fall out?*

Today was not going to be that day. I grimaced and scowled as I looked at the cotton maternity pad; it was creased and disfigured from my movement whilst asleep. Today, it was speckled with a snot-coloured residue.

Day '*something*'.

My heart sank; I sighed heavily. Today was not the day 'we' would reach victory. It was not the day that I could truly get back on track and get on with my recovery. Instead, with a heavy heart and a resigned, tortured, beaten body, I drag myself out of bed, putting on a fake smile, ready to face whatever happens next.

A Day in the Life

Each day post-surgery is a fantastic voyage of discovery. With the very real problems of a successful operation but complicated recovery, it's really difficult to exude body confidence, to show that vim and vigour and confidence I showed before the time came. The actual operation itself is relatively nondescript. You arrive at the hospital, get settled, get changed, sign the consent form and then await being wheeled to theatre. Sometime later you wake up. In my case, the first words I said when I came to was that I needed a pee. I had a catheter so my body took care of itself.

Hospital was uneventful. The food was amazing, though – world-class. There was some leaking but nothing too distressing, and the week flew by. There was nothing much in the way of pain, just soreness, and the only real jolt was when the drain, the catheter and then the packing was taken out. It really is the most odd thing to see and feel as something is collected out of your insides, and the smell will haunt me for some time.

I made it out of hospital relatively unscathed, though an infection I didn't yet realize I had was beginning. My parents had driven to pick me up, flanked by a multitude of things I never needed to take or use, and two 'not so small' dilators – eek! Days would have to be planned and a schedule maintained, even if it was the last thing I wanted to do. The time off needed for recovery would be my first proper break from life in some time. For years I have gone on and on like a Duracell Bunny, doing anything and everything I possibly could now that the post-transition world had removed the barriers that held back me from doing and achieving all that I wanted.

Dilation, though, would throw a spanner into that much like the Luddites would do to new-fangled machinery. This thing would bring everything to a slower, controlled pace, restricting that once magnificent world view. Sure my body was recovering, sure 'we' were fighting off the most stubborn of infections and sure I would be scaring myself half to death finding new and exciting bits of me in my pad. Dilation, though, is utterly relentless.

Many moons ago, I went through IVF with a partner. It didn't work, and you as a reader don't need to know that part of it; however, there is a certain part of it that relates exactly to dilation. At one point of the IVF process, there is a period where you and your partner have to have sex every two days, come what may. Two is the optimum time for a number of factors; however, it is utterly relentless. If you are both tired, sex. If you both don't feel particularly sexy, sex. If you both would rather do a million and one other different things, sex. And so on.

Dilation is not that different. Come rain, sleet, wind or snow? Dilation. Coronavirus? That's dilation. UTI and kidney stones? Dilation. I actually missed a day's dilation because of a paramedic call-out for pain, fever, discharge and then a subsequent A&E visit. Next day, though – you guessed it – dilation! Each surgeon has different requirements; however, for at least the first eight weeks 'we' have had to dilate three times a day, every day. It doesn't matter if I am feeling shitty, or I want to rest, or in most cases I just want to sleep as recovery is exhausting. I still have to set aside time to dilate.

Each session takes anywhere from 30 to 45 minutes depending on how much preparation I have to do. Clean dilators, set up my 'dilation station', find wet wipes to rub off the slippery lube from my hands which are already battered from all of the washing because of Coronavirus. Then 'we' need to be still for 20–30 minutes. Two different dilators, two different circumferences. Smallest first for a short time and then the larger one for the rest.

During that time, you can do not much. It's not 'lying on your back thinking of England', nor is it a particularly pleasurable experience. Sure the celebration of 'Yesssssss! I have a vagina!' is immense; however, it soon makes way to 'For fuck's sake! Dilation again? Fuck my life!' For those 20–30 minutes whilst the dilators are inside you, there is very little you can do. I've meditated, listened to music, watched wrestling and other TV shows. I have mentally listed all of the things I'd rather be doing than going through this again, solved world hunger, vanquished the 'Demons of Galaxitar', daydreamed, planned out my life and everything in between. However, there's that nagging sense of dread that once this session is over and 'we' have prepped for the next one, then, as night follows day, I will be dilating again, in just a few short hours. Just like the Duracell Bunny I was before, I have had to change the batteries and start up again. I am tired and I have no idea at this point how I manage to keep going. These are some amazing power cells; either that or I am the Terminator and will not stop, ever, apparently.

Thoughts from a Dark Place

It's late, days have passed since I last sat down to write; however, the reasons for that surround an increased ennui at my seemingly never-ending situation. 'We' are still fighting infection, 'we' are still on antibiotics and 'we' are still in the midst of an almighty struggle to get fit and back to work.

No one really speaks about things not going right after Gender Reassignment Surgery. Sure, the potential danger and complications are spelt out before surgery and when you give consent. However, from those who have gone through it, there is usually an expectation that everything is 'pink fluffy clouds' and a culmination of their life's work to achieve that which has alluded them for so long. It is immensely liberating to finally have a body that looks vaguely as it is supposed to. It is not time to break out the ticker-tape parade, though, nor is it time to celebrate like life's work is completed, done.

There are and can be complications from this surgery; add in dilation, and then recovery, and 'we' are still fighting. Every day is a struggle to not go backwards, in the desperate hope that someday 'we' can start moving forwards. Trans people fight so many things. We fight our minds, our body, for our right to change, our right to be, our right to have equal rights, our right to be accepted and our right to be free. This fight is just another in a very long list of things to overcome. You don't need to have surgery to be you, and it's not for everyone, as it means more changes and perhaps, not unsurprisingly, more fighting. Sometimes it's easy to imagine yourself as a 'war-weary' sergeant from the trenches of WWI.

Just one more trip over the top, I thought, waiting for the shells to start crashing all around me, the whistles signalling the start of yet another full-blown conflict where I can't be sure I'd survive.

Just one! If I can make it through this battle alive, then I can return back to civilian life. No more intense battles, no more dragging this tired body and mind through No Man's Land. No more, ever!

Alas, each and every time, I manage to barely make it through the waves of attacks. Soon enough, I will be standing, tired, dishevelled and a bit more run-down, ready to fight again!

I wrote about this oft-unexplored part of trans life because 'we' are told we should be ecstatic, 'we' should have whatever other expectations of the collective glee that others think we should have. I am glad to finally be able to have some kind of vaguely acceptable vessel to carry my essence in. It beats having one I utterly loathe and it is a massive step up. Dilation and infection, though, will not bring you pages and pages of Google hits, nor will it bring you the secret to life or how to cope if you cough or sneeze whilst dilating. For all of the 'amazing' things about being trans, these aspects are ignored, not covered, or, even more alarmingly, do not seem to exist.

With that in mind, I can't celebrate. Not yet. It's for my renewed body to celebrate, when I am ready, or if indeed want to. Infection and dilation have sucked a lot of my power, my passion and my drive out of me, and recovering during a global pandemic was also not in the manual when I signed up to this.

It's not something to be lauded, celebrated by others on your behalf, and I'm not incredibly brave (that is so overused!). I'm finally getting to be me for me. Chary, punch-drunk and not sure of what day it is, I take my broken, battered and shell-shocked body off to bed. I lie down with my thoughts starting to race about tomorrow. Ready, waiting, expectant. 'We' shall rise to fight again!

Banana

Harry Mizumoto

It's raining today. I overslept and the inside of my mouth is gummy with sleep. Still, the pale white of the window rinses the room with light, and for the first time in a while I feel calm. I pad into the kitchen to find something to eat. The tiles greet me with bits of dust which stick to the soles of my naked feet. A stack of plates sit patiently in the sink. Instead of going through the hassle of washing or heating anything, I opt for a banana, plucking a yellow curve from its taper of green stalks. It's bitter and I regret my choice. Eating the under-ripe fruit, I'm reminded of a passage in the early pages of *Pond*,[1] in which the

---

1   Claire-Louise Bennett, Fitzcarraldo Editions, London, 2015.

protagonist – unnamed, solitary, living in some Irish village – hands out advice on the nature of a good breakfast. 'A banana should be accompanied by bitter coffee', I paraphrase, since I don't have the book to consult or pore over, and this phrase patterns over my thoughts like the faint plinks of rain on glass.

There's a lot of fruit in that book – bouncing about and exerting contrasts – pulsing through a first-person narration waxing lyrical on benign activities like chopping watermelons, taking a walk, planting, complaining to neighbors, etc. It feels criminal just to list these actions because they're intensified in the midst of acute solitude, unwrapped from their tidy names and engulfed in textures all juxtaposed like silk on leather. This anonymizing makes it possible to detach the protagonist from unwieldy titles like 'woman' or 'academic'. The protagonist is weird, funny, lightly misanthropic. She wages a war on words – 'My native language isn't English, but something more private and internal', she says, or something like that – so we talk in the linguistic typology of the garden, through the red-ripe sheen of tomatoes, the dirt filing under polished fingernails, the potato peels saved in a bowl for compost. The protagonist doesn't subjugate her surroundings with words, but becomes it.

Meanwhile, social distancing is aseptic. I spend hours looking/tapping at screens. I blink in and out of sleep, while anxiety numbs my wrists. Fabric chafes my skin. I scrub. I think too much. Recently, it feels like everything is separated from me by a pane of glass.

My banana is too bitter to justify a coffee, so I abandon the idea and ooze back into bed. I think vaguely of thumbs splitting mandarins, fresh juice cutting through 'the fugue of sex'...easy, baby, easy.

*

As in Spanish or French, every German noun has a gender. While Romance languages only have two grammatical genders, in German the definite article 'the' comes in three flavors: *der* (male), *die* (female) or *das* (neutral). The neutral form is reserved for objects. People with jobs are paired like neat hetero couples: teachers are either *der Lehrer*, the male teacher, or *die Lehrerin*, the female teacher. It's grammatically incorrect to refer to a teacher without his or her gender.

In the first few weeks of German class, my female professor told us a riddle about a surgeon. It goes like this:

Q. A father and son get into a car crash. The father dies at the scene. The son is rushed to hospital and taken to the operating room. The surgeon says: I can't operate on this boy, he's my son.

How is this possible?

A. The surgeon is the boy's mother.

Her point was that this gender bias riddle doesn't work in German because the surgeon would be gendered: *die Chirurgin*. She spoke about sexism and ingrained stereotypes, about professors she worked alongside who were condescended to for being *die Professorin* instead of the totemic *der*. My professor's feminism was relatively uncontroversial: white and cis-gendered, rooted in traditional concerns like the wage gap instead of the gender binary. So what about us?

I read a study on German gender-fair language. A university student asked her German-speaking and genderqueer peers how they navigated their gender identity in a language in which gender is unavoidable and most labels on gender and sexual orientation are pejorative.

They said they spoke English.

*

In 2009, my family and I moved from the US to Japan, when I was nine and my sister was seven. Since our Japanese was worse than our burgeoning English, we were enrolled at an international Catholic all-girls school. This was two years before the Tōhoku earthquake, three years before my *Oji-chan* passed away, and four years before I twisted into shapes I didn't know how to explain.

The private school I attended was a bubble of well-rounded *Ojousans* (read: rich young ladies) prepped to major in marketing at USC or Georgetown. The small, close-knit community prided itself on its progressive and feminist spirit, offering a rigorous program with a host of extracurricular sports. Our slogan was 'Once a Sacred Heart girl, always a Sacred Heart girl'. The 'girl' part, obviously, was par for the course. In the meantime, I kept myself busy with a steady diet of pirated American shows and books in English, operating as if I'd never left the temperate climate of southern California.

In eighth grade, I learned I was a boy by cutting my hair and starting Tumblr. While Lizzie McGuire huffed around freshman year in distressed jeans and organza, I wore baggy sweatshirts and slouched to hide my chest. No one knew about my identity except my best friend. I hated going to barber shops so I cut my own hair over Skype, consulting her while snipping at myself in the mirror.

Where should I cut next? Does it look okay?

Maybe a bit in the front, it's uneven there. But it looks really good!

It looked terrible. Afterwards my mom dragged me to a professional salon to get a proper haircut, and I received a slick Asian bowl cut. My sister said I looked like a K-pop star. As the only student with cropped hair and illegal pants – usually only acceptable in the winter – I stuck out. Somehow this earned me an unofficial fan club. The girls in my grade took turns asking me to wink at them, screaming when I did. I was flattered, but also confused – was this gay? Did they like me? Or were they just teasing me, making fun of how I looked? Back then I didn't think I could be attractive; I only saw what I lacked.

*

Three Ali Smith novels later, I moved to London. I changed my name to something masculine so I could be girly and mess with people. When strangers meet me at parties, they ask if my name's short for something. I say no and smile. Watching people get confused never fails to be amusing.

I was selective about who I explained my gender to. Most of the time, the gender confusion of my name felt like enough. I knew that the statements 'I'm non-binary' or 'my pronouns are they/them' wouldn't have been conclusive, and would unleash a flurry of questions that I wouldn't have the energy to answer. Sometimes it's easier to stay silent. I perceive my gender as something private, internal.

My ex took some pictures of me lying naked. He showed them to me afterwards, happy that he had created something aesthetically pleasing. I was dismayed. The picture was dark, illuminated by a single lamp. The harsh contrast exaggerated the round lumps of my body, curving limply over the bed. I'll delete them once we break up, he said. We broke up a week later.

I just didn't recognize that body. It didn't look like the one I saw in the mirror, frontal and upright, strictly two-dimensional. The only gaze was mine.

*

I'm trying to write about my gender, but it's been difficult. I can only write in fragments, snatches of memory and feeling. Writing this way is painful. I write snippets, ranging from a single line to a paragraph, which I'm left to weave into a coherent whole.

How do you write about something you don't have the words for – something that specifically defies language? I tread that mean boy–girl terrain in a world where such distinctions don't exist. I used to bandage and hide my body, because its dimensions didn't sit right in the definitions, didn't checkmark the terms and conditions. Now, my body is genderless, because it's mine and I said so. I'm getting used to living with it. The best and hardest part is volleying, of eluding shape and grammar, gliding through world as fragments pieced together. I want to choose a level of communication that isn't verbal but something lower; something kinesthetic, floral or metallic, like pottery bound together with *kintsugi*, the way き lies halfway between 'kiss' and 'Keats'. There's a language in me I'm trying, itching, reaching to free. I just need to learn the words.

Torso

Kole Fulmine

One arm – normally the right – supermans up overhead; the other draws downwards, gripping and then sliding unnoticeably through; body turns to greet, twisting from the hips, and the left arm tucks upwards close to the ribs, popping a thumb. Deftly hooking and wrenching bunched-up fabric into a neat line along the length of the bone, head furrows almost violently through, closed eyes (every time) and pull, gently at first; to establish boundaries, the stretchy part is safe-zoned for stronger tugs. This bit, the stretchy bit, should sit flat on the back and so is the first part that the arm – usually the left – extends backwards to the base of the neck to grasp, fingers contorted, push up, look up, body fully taut – thank fuck for yoga – inhale, again, one swift tug is all that it needs to settle into place, exhale. Now, two fingers on each hand desperately (because the back part has taken quite some time and exposure to the elements has to be reduced to roughly 30 seconds) seek out the double panel, firm pieces of cotton that have been overstitched along the seams to provide additional support. Fronted with a shiny, nylon fabric, similar in texture to clothing labels; the breast plate, the protective covering that can be smoothed down once everything is safe. This part is the hardest pull, because it hurts. Still it must be done and so, with an even deeper breath and a final downwards motion that means the rest of the day will be just better, the front is fully secured over the chest. Bending over to firmly swipe each nipple to a central position so that an even flatness can be presented. Shoulders are pulled back for final inspection in front of the mirror – the only full look the body is permitted; criticisms clumsily stack into one another and distract from what's important: the chest is now bound. This part of every day is easier to bear if it can be done only once; the worst is in hot weather when multiple show-ers are required. What would a waterproof binder look like? A binder that never had to be removed, a freedom that can't be imagined, as a familiar, swelling tingle of despair begins to jut deep into the pit of the stomach – 24 hours is never enough time to have to do this all over again.

The fourth photograph in the series sits directly over a white radiator in my bathroom. So that when I stack my towel or when I brush my teeth and stare absentmindedly into the mirror, it is the photograph that I ingest most intently. My gaze could be described at that moment in that obsequious way one would ascribe to a lover. Or maybe it's more lusty than that; nevertheless, it is desirous. Desire to have and to hold, not the man, but the object itself. If only it were mine.

I purchased my first binder over a year ago and closed the door to anyone, especially my ex-partner, seeing my naked body again. Those wobbly, fleshy sacks of oxytocin that sit high on my rib cage do not belong to me and therefore cannot be seen. They are an addition that I did not ask for. And all the meaning, all the hidden meaning that is imbued into this body part can go fuck itself. To bind means that my clothes look suitably androgynous. In between, a not-either status is confirmed when strangers' eyes surreptitiously greet the chest and are met with flatness. To present a nothingness is, of course, impossible. Because there is always something, always flattened body parts. No matter how tight I bind, there is a fleshy mound that accumulates near the armpits, impossible to disguise. The options to avoid this clumsy clumping are too painful, too expensive to consider, so this will do. Against better judgement, I long for the chill, the wintery thrill of being able to wear jumpers, because thicker layers mean that the eyes are distracted from that place.

There are four photographs on my bathroom wall, measuring roughly six by four inches. Framed in white metal and arranged in a way that feels slightly pretentious. The artist's name I know because of his monthly newsletters that surreptitiously burden my inbox. I try to push him out of my mind when I look up at them daily. A friendly enough guy, he is one of those people you wouldn't want to have a drink with in the pub because his awkwardness brings out your awkwardness and you end up talking about really mundane things like the weather. The first of the series, starting from the left, is a cloud-streaked sky. There are three streaks of white and the background is blue, only it's tinged with a hyperreal pink on the edges. Nothing more, nothing less. The second is dusty pink and salmon, with sharp bursts of white, a rectangle of colour, shot as if someone were taking a photo of a screen with their phone. It vibrates slightly, creating a blurred tonal range. The third – surreal with a nineties undertone, could also be a screenshot – is of a man walking in the sun with a small child on his shoulders. The man has sunglasses on and the girl is wearing a swimming costume. The effect is a mirage; a beautifully hot, shimmering landscape. All three make me feel a bit trippy and, when I'm hungover, can be challenging. The final in the series is the real reason for my particular interest in these photographs. It is an image of a chest. A flattened, tanned chest. The person in the image is bending towards the camera and has therefore been decapitated so that the chest is the central focus of the shot. It fills the four corners of the print. In oranges and muted tones of umber, two nipples float centrally and there is some definition to the torso – arms outstretched – which is cut at the waistline by a pair of washed-out blue denim jeans.

I don't really even question why it's OK to be judged so brazenly based on two mounds of fat that furnish this part of my body. Why is it OK that this rise and dip, this mountain range that flumps and bounces about can be the place that gathers all of me up in one swift answer: female. That which sits on the front of my body can connote how I am engaged with, categorized, filed and processed: woman. All the mess of the in-between disappears as soon as others catch a glimpse of that undulating region: girl. Because from just underneath my tits, my stomach is ruler-ish and straight. My hips are narrower than my shoulders. Arms toned, somewhat defined, wrists are a little skinny, hands larger than average. Arse – well, that area is a continual battle; forcing it to become firmer, flatter, non-existent – if only that area could be bound up too. Legs androgynously shaped and feet are wide and long enough to be affectionately termed 'hobbit-like', so that the only shoes I can fit into are invariably categorized as belonging to men. Even my face has a certain ambiguity to it, meaning in certain lights and at certain points of any given day I am mistaken for 'Sir'.

The short bursts of negative vibrations on my electric toothbrush mean I have been, yet again, staring for 90 seconds. Who does this chest belong to? River Phoenix, Christian Slater, Patrick Swayze, Keanu Reeves...their chests so brazenly determining a freedom in clothing that sits almost perfectly. Idolized since forever. In that moment I disconnect from my body, the one that stares back at me, and it is in here that I capture all that desire, all that freedom. Understanding the essence of what I would most happily change about this body. To walk around shirtless and fancy-free is something that will never happen in my lifetime because the scars would be, well, too harsh, and that is something I would never be able to mask. That the confusion of that chest placed on this body would be a collage too hard to glue down, the frilly edges of the cut-up would always come unstuck in public places, and maybe even not so public places. So I stare and I use this daily moment of sweet release, of complete and utter reprieve, to brush my teeth and set myself up for the greatest disappointment of all.

My Amazing Mostly Monochrome Dreamcoat

Ezra Woodger

When asked to write something about my every-day experience as a trans person, it's tempting to dig up the sad stuff. Coming-out stories. The tears. The six-year waiting list, the self-harm, anorexia, the cruel snarl of a stranger as I wipe his spit from my face.

But instead, I want to talk about Isaac.

I used to wear a statement jacket, from the ages of about 16 to a few months back. There's been a spike in transphobia recently, and I felt safer leaving it at home. I could go on about my complex relationship with that dilemma, but maybe that's for another time. This jacket was covered in slogans and pins: 'punks not dead', 'gay liberation front', 'Nazi Punks Fuck Off'. The back was reserved for the largest patch, haphazardly stitched with white thread, a DIY piece I'd bought from a gig held for a local transgender charity. In block lettering it read, 'TRANS PUNKS: SMASH THE CIS-TEM'.

I thought it was brilliant, and it made me feel powerful to wear it. I knew it was a literal target on my back – I was brash, not stupid – but it didn't seem to matter that much. It meant that when people misgendered me, I could bite back. The more obvious I made it, the more intentional their hatred became. It was easier to deal with if I could see it happening. Transphobia is a strange creature in that the parts that hurt the most are sometimes the most benign, and I found the general assumption that I was a girl really difficult to deal with. Obviously. Baring my teeth and growling out a 'fuck you' to anyone who refused to respect me despite being given the opportunity to was far less terrifying than having to hide a furious, humiliated blush and mumble out, 'Uh, he.' Putting on the jacket was putting on armor. People were going to stare at me regardless (yes, cis people, we can see you), so I might as well pretend it was because I looked cool. I suppose it's refreshing to feel like I don't have to wear it anymore.

I've had too many comments on that jacket to

remember them all. Mostly drunk people in clubs fawning over how rad it is. I remember one man asked for my name and promised to look me up on Facebook when he got home. I told him, but only because I was absolutely certain that he wasn't going to remember it. I never heard from him, so I guess I was right. Sometimes people took it as a challenge: 'You aren't a guy. No, you aren't! No way!'

I remember having to hold my two (cis girl) friends back from clawing a woman's eyes out on my behalf. Violence, verbal or physical, just seemed like a constant and real threat that hung over me, visible just on the edge of my field of vision. If you wear glasses, it kind of feels like when your eyes get used to seeing the frames so phase them out from what you can see, but sometimes you become weirdly hyperaware of them being there. Just in front of your nose.

It had been a few weeks since the 'spit in face' occurrence briefly referenced at the beginning of this story. It had shaken me, as it had everyone who was there at the time. I've written a poem about it; my friend mentioned that he had stopped holding his boyfriend's hand for a while after. We were all coping in our own quiet ways. It was one of the few times I'd seriously considered cutting the patch off the back of my jacket. He had overheard us talking, and that was the catalyst, but what if he had seen it? Would the attack have been worse? Would I have put the people I love in danger? The concept struck me more than it would have if my own life had been the only one on the line. I didn't like thinking that my actions were putting the people around me at risk. Of course, I wasn't the only one with LGBT patches on my jacket. We are a bunch of queers, after all. But the responsibility weighed on me. Middle-child syndrome, maybe.

I was sitting outside the station on a cool autumn day. I didn't like to loiter there, as that had been the location of the event, but I needed to pause and roll a cigarette. I was a pretty heavy smoker back then, and my need for nicotine trumped just about every other instinct I had. So I sat on one of the concrete blocks and began my little ritual, shivering slightly in the chill. I carefully measured tobacco out on to the paper, being careful to not get it caught in the breeze.

'Excuse me...'

The voice made me jump, I can remember. I don't get approached by strangers in broad daylight all that often. Especially not when I'm rolling a cigarette. For a brief, terrible moment, I think it's a sibling, and standing behind them will be my mum, and, oh fuck, she is going to *kill* me if she finds out I smoke. But the person hovering at my side isn't anyone I know. Their hair is light, slightly curled. They look about 15 years old. I smile, as friendly as possible. Maybe they're lost. Maybe I'm sitting on something of theirs and I didn't notice. Maybe...

'I just wanted to say I really like your jacket,' they say in a small voice. I relax, even though I hadn't been aware of the sudden tension that bolted my entire body upright. I can now be certain I'm not at risk. Hate crimes, or the disappointment of my mother. Both were bad.

'Thank you!' I lick my cigarette closed and tuck it behind my ear for a moment. 'I made some of the patches myself.'

Their eyes widen. 'That's really cool!' There is a small but noticeable pause. 'I especially like the back one.'

I smile again, prepared for it to go a number of different ways. They open their mouth. Fuck, I hope this isn't going to be weird. I pray that this kid doesn't make it weird.

'I'm a trans guy, but my family is really bad so I can't come out to them, but I saw your patch and wanted to come and say hello, and thank you, and hello.'

It all comes out in a rush. He tells me his dead-name, but I forget it as soon as it leaves his lips. He introduces himself as Isaac, and he thanks me for existing.

I can't help it, I pull him into a hug. With permission, of course. I hold his shoulders and I tell him that one day he's going to be able to be himself, unapologetically, and I am already so proud of him. We part ways and I can't stop smiling, almost (but not quite) forgetting the cigarette behind my ear.

He probably doesn't remember me now, but I remember him. With one small, incredibly brave act, Isaac reminded me why I wore that scruffy old jacket. Why I was so loud about my identity, why I was running for Head Boy at sixth form despite complaints from other students, why I would never hide because of old neo-Nazi fucks who get a kick out of spitting at teenagers for being happy. Isaac had seen someone like him and had felt safe enough to share a part of himself with a complete stranger. I had made him feel safe. Regardless of what kind of home life waited for him, in that moment he had felt able to be himself.

I remember Isaac because I used to be him.

I think about how much it would have helped me to see people like me existing, and being happy and whole and human. When I was first coming to terms with who I am, the only representation I could find was *Boys Don't Cry*. I got ten minutes in and couldn't continue; I knew how it ended, and I didn't want to think it could end like that for me. My best friend at the time was upset because she had wanted to watch it with me. I didn't have the heart to tell her that I couldn't handle watching it with someone cis.

But imagine if I had seen someone in the street who was like me. Someone in a dirty old jacket, the ends of the sleeves turned grey from smoke. If you look at it close enough, you'd be able to see the parts that weren't sewn on properly out of laziness. A jacket that loudly and proudly told me that I wasn't alone.

I realized the real reason I wore it everywhere I went wasn't to catch transphobes in the act, although that was a bonus of sorts. I realized I could be the person that made people feel safe. I could be exactly the kind of man I needed growing up. And that was worth all the harassment and awkward encounters in the whole world.

I understand that this story isn't actually very interesting. I wore a jacket outside and had a conversation with a stranger. But recently I've sworn off telling people the juicy parts of my life. Cis people can find

somewhere else to get their trauma porn. Trans people go through so much, but the smallest of victories
can sometimes stay with us the longest. The first time
we use the right toilet. The first time we use the right
changing room. Our first pair of our own shoes. I've
since moved to university and started HRT, but I still
haven't forgotten about Isaac. I hope he's doing okay,
and is safe. I'm proud of him no matter what.

Sometimes pride isn't smashing a bottle through
the Houses of Parliament. Sometimes it's making your
own home, just for a moment, and through it you can
find your own family. I'm so incredibly honoured to
have a family so diverse and beautiful, and I'm even
more honoured to have kids like Isaac in it.

Afterword

Dr Jay Stewart, CEO, Gendered Intelligence

'Transition' is an important term and concept at Gendered Intelligence and indeed across our trans and gender diverse communities. It can mean many different things to different people and its meaning has shifted and changed over time. Like all terms it is culturally specific but also transitioning itself can differ across cultures, histories, countries and communities in accordance with what is possible and what is known to be possible by each individual.

Transition broadly describes the actions a person takes to move away from the assumed or given gender we each receive by institutions, established practices and norms and to move towards another gender. To depart from one's birth gender and towards something else can, in broad terms, be what it means to be trans.

In the not-too-distant past, transition referred mostly to the actions taken that are often described as 'medical' – that is to say to receive hormone therapy and/or surgical intervention. Transition was understood in more narrow terms – that of changing one's body. At Gendered Intelligence (GI), over the past decade we have encouraged others to place more focus on a trans person's social transition. These are the actions that a person takes socially, interactively in the world. They include aspects such as using a different pronoun, perhaps going by a different name, expressing one's gender differently through hair, clothes, make up, behaviour, voice quality – a whole array of things. Social transition can also involve amendments to identity documents such as passports and driving licences. The reason for encouraging a focus on social transition links to the desire to live in a world with increased opportunity, acceptance and celebration of diverse, sometimes nonconforming, actions or behaviours. Moreover, if those others around trans people can adapt, accept and respect our requests, desires and needs – for instance, to use a different pronoun and name – then medical transitions will be considered less primary, less at the forefront, of people's understanding of what it means to be trans.

This then moves away from the invasive curiosity others have about trans bodies and what we choose to do with them. If we are to deem medical matters to be private, then it is no business of others. This kind of thinking reframes being trans and transitioning away from a medical model and more to a social model.

The trans movement has learnt a lot from the social model of disability that stipulates 'it is not my body that is wrong – it is the world around us that is wrong in that it is not accommodating of my body.'[1]

In some countries across the globe, trans people can legally transition. That means to be legally recognized in our gender. Legally transitioning is not something all trans people can do – depending on the nation's legislation that is in place, but also it might depend on whether a person can afford it, or if they have the right paperwork, or if they are the right age. Indeed, not all trans people wish to legally transition. Yet there is an important politic around who it is that determines our gender – is it the medical establishment, the state or ourselves?

---

1   Scope (2021) 'Social model of disability.' www.scope.org.uk/about-us/social-model-of-disability.

There is also an idea that we emotionally or psychologically transition. This describes the self-discovery, the deep reflections that trans people take, be it prior to or indeed throughout, the point at which actions or articulations are taken that shares, shifts, and shapes their gender in ways that differ or depart from what has so far been assumed and given. Psychological transitioning forces us to ask the big questions – Who am I? What do I want? What do I need to live and feel alive in my body, in my mind, in this world?

Over recent years, transition has become a term that has broadened in its scope. There are many ways to transition and no way is the right way. Each trans person can pick and choose what is right for them in any given moment. A trans person can have more than one transition. Transition is not a one-way track.

Trans, non-binary, gender questioning and gender diverse people face a number of significant inequalities, including higher levels of discrimination, shame, abuse and violence; greater inequalities in health and wellbeing, especially mental health; higher levels of social isolation, exclusion and loneliness; and less opportunity in terms of education, training and employment. The causes of these inequalities are many and complex but are ultimately underpinned by poor understandings of gender, the reductive thinking and reinforcement of the 'gender binary' and social pressures to conform to gender norms (and the consequences experienced if you don't).

At GI we imagine a world where diverse gender identities and expressions are visible and valued, and where trans, non-binary, gender diverse and gender questioning people can live healthy, safe and fulfilled lives. We are working towards this by focusing on increasing understandings of gender diversity and in improving the quality of life of trans, non-binary, gender diverse and gender questioning people. Where we use the term 'trans', it is intended to describe the broad spectrum of people who feel that their assigned sex at birth does not describe who they are. This includes, but is not limited to, non-binary, gender queer or gender questioning, trans men/trans masculine people, trans women/trans feminine people and men and women with a trans history. We believe that exploring gender is positive for everyone, including cisgender people (people who aren't trans).

Established in 2008, Gendered Intelligence is a trans led and trans involving organization – there are many trans identified people working at all levels in the organization. We respect that trans people's lives are rich and diverse, including their gender identity, sexuality, age, race and ethnicity, faith and beliefs, class and socio-economic background, disabilities and abilities. We therefore proactively aim to offer opportunities that reflect, value and are accessible to people with those diverse experiences.

If Gendered Intelligence wishes to fulfil its mission and have a lasting impact then we need to work with depth and breadth across key areas of life – from the micro to the macro. The value that we offer, as Gendered Intelligence, is significant, not least because of the ways in which we work across multiple sectors and have multiple perspectives. We deliver Youth and Community Services, including youth groups, events and residentials; we have parent and carer groups, telephone helpline and online support service, mentoring for trans people in education, a volunteer scheme, a network for activists (GIANTS), and we deliver a range of community arts/heritage/ cultural projects as well as group therapy for adults. Our Professional and Educational Services include delivering training for professionals, consultancy including policy work, presentations, keynotes and panel discussions and we run assemblies, workshops and lectures in the education sector. We also run a Therapists and Counsellors Network. Our Public Engagement work involves carrying out of research, effecting public policy and influencing decision makers and responding to and influencing the media.

Through the range of activities that we carry out we know that we present a wider picture of lived experience of gender diversity – we are not only delivering services, nor are we only doing educative work of increasing understanding, but we are also committed to effecting policy and shifting cultural behaviours through engaging with the wider general public, including the media and government. This brings certain complexities to us as an organization, and, whilst it is not easy, it is important to hold these multiple positions and perspectives.

Each of these aspects informs one another and it is our USP at Gendered Intelligence that we learn from members of our community, especially our young people, and implement that learning across the organization.

At Gendered Intelligence we want to see a paradigm shift in the way society thinks about gender. A key way to improve the lives of gender diverse people is to change hearts and minds and this is done so effectively through the act of storytelling. But we also need to think carefully about which stories are told, to whom, and for what reasons. It's important that we empower individuals to tell their own stories in way that is right for them and where they feel they have full agency over them. At GI, we resist victim-based stories of gender diverse experiences but instead platform stories that are rich, varied and intersectional lived experiences had in our communities.

This book *Transitions: Our Stories of Being Trans* does that. The stories of the everyday in this anthology are bold and strong. They show the diversity and multiplicity of trans identities, but also of the desire to be visible, and to challenge assumptions. They refer to our heritage; to our cultural inheritance. They talk of trans as being beyond and going above and beyond for each other. They talk about the vital importance of our 'fellow travellers', of our community. Transition is a process and the process continues; there is no 'ticker-tape parade', as one of the stories points out; we are never 'done' or finished. And so, neither is our work at Gendered Intelligence. We will continue to work hard to ensure that all gender diverse people feel appreciated, celebrated and connected.

Contributor Biographies

Den Casey is a proud non-binary lesbian in their early sixties. They have worked for many years in health administration. They live happily with their long-term partner, two cats and two dogs, and their interests include travel, DIY and vegan cookery. This is their first published writing project.

Kole Fulmine is a PhD candidate at Roehampton University. They use a hybrid of autofiction, critical theory and poetry to engage with neutrality. As a fully qualified personal trainer, they work with queer bodies in an attempt to understand the more intimate complexity of trans life narratives.

Danielle Hopkins is something of an old hand at life. There isn't much she hasn't been able to overcome. About to take up a national role following a successful interview, she hopes that her work resonates with the reader so that they can see what the hidden trans everyday looks and feels like.

Kirrin Medcalf loves all creatures on four legs and all things green and wild, yet perplexingly they live in London, after ending up there searching for queerer shores. They share a flat with their hamster Loki and many furbys. They have a smorgasbord of a CV, having worked as a violence survivors' advocate, a trans youth worker, a sexual health assistant, a historical reenactment tutor, and a lecturer in criminology. They dabble in nature writing, poetry, photography, weaving and crafting. They aim to bring their experiences as a trans, queer and neurodiverse person to all their art.

Harry Mizumoto is a writer and artist based in London. They are co-running the non-profit queer publishing house and art collective, POLARI Print (@polariprint), and editing the Comparative Lit. focused journal, SUBTEXT. They have two dogs and a goldfish.

Tash Oakes-Monger works in LGBT health and writes whenever they can. They mainly write poetry about a variety of things including queerness, friendship and being trans.

Edward Whelan lives in London with a stripy ginger cat. He can usually be found cycling through the woods.

Ezra Woodger is a writer from the East of England. He is the father of one very lazy cat and has a passion for horror movies. He has performed poetry at various local live events, but has recently shifted attention to non-fiction and activist work.

Trans Everyday –
Your Experience

....

....

....

....

....

....

....

....

....

TRANSITIONS

Trans Love

An Anthology of Transgender
and Non-Binary Voices

Edited by Freiya Benson

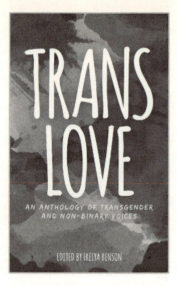

**Selected as a 2019 LGBT Book
of the Year by *Dazed* and
Ms. Magazine.**

A ground-breaking anthology
of writing on the topic of love,
written by trans and non-binary people who share their
thoughts, feelings and experiences of love in all its guises.
The collection spans familial,
romantic, spiritual and self-
love as well as friendships and ally love, to provide a broad
and honest understanding of how trans people navigate love
and relationships, and what love means to them.

Reclaiming what love means to trans people, this book
provokes conversations that are not reflected in what is pres-
ently written, moving the narrative around trans identities
away from sensationalism. At once intimate and radical, and
both humorous and poignant, this book is for anyone who has
loved, who is in love, and who is looking for love.

Freiya Benson is a trans woman and an experienced writer,
and has written for magazines and websites, including the
Huffington Post and *Vice*.

£14.99 | $19.95 | PB | 296PP | ISBN 978 1 78592 432 3 | EISBN 978 1 78450 804 3

Life Isn't Binary

On Being Both, Beyond, and In-Between

Meg-John Barker and Alex Iantaffi

Foreword by CN Lester

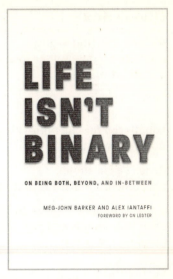

'The book we all need for this moment in time' – CN Lester

This ground-breaking book looks at how non-binary methods of thought can be applied to all aspects of life, and offer new and greater ways of understanding ourselves and how we relate to others.

Using bisexual and non-binary gender experiences as a starting point, this book addresses the key issues with binary thinking regarding our relationships, bodies, emotions, wellbeing and our sense of identity and sets out a range of practices which may help us to think in more non-binary, both/and, or uncertain ways.

A truly original and insightful piece, this guide encourages reflection on how we view and understand the world we live in and how we all bend, blur or break society's binary codes.

Meg-John Barker is an internationally recognised and hugely influential writer, therapist and thinker on gender, sex, relationships and mental health.

Alex Iantaffi is an internationally recognized independent scholar, speaker and writer on issues of gender, disability, sexuality and mental health.

£14.99 | $19.95 | PB | 240PP | ISBN 978 1 78592 479 8 | EISBN 978 1 78450 864 7

Queer Sex

A Trans and Non-Binary
Guide to Intimacy, Pleasure
and Relationships

Juno Roche

**Longlisted for the Polari First
Book Prize 2019.**

'Queer Sex is simply
phenomenal' – Bitch Media

'A gift to anyone looking to
open their minds and fall
in love' – CN Lester

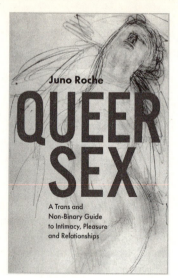

In this frank, funny and poignant book, transgender activist
Juno Roche discusses sex, desire and dating with leading figures from the trans and non-binary community.

Calling out prejudices and inspiring readers to explore
their own concepts of intimacy and sexuality, the first-hand
accounts celebrate the wonder and potential of trans bodies
and push at the boundaries of how society views gender, sexuality and relationships.

Empowering and necessary, this collection shows all trans
people deserve to feel brave, beautiful and sexy.

Juno Roche is an internationally recognised trans writer and
campaigner, and Founder of Trans Workers UK and the Trans
Teachers Network. On the Independent's Rainbow List 2015
and 2016, she is a patron of cliniQ and contributes to publica-
tions including *Diva*, *The Guardian* and *Vice*.

£12.99 | $18.95 | PB | 168PP | ISBN 978 1 78592 406 4 | EISBN 978 1 78450 770 1

Trans Power

Own Your Gender

Juno Roche

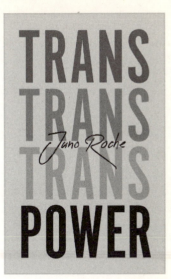

Shortlisted for the Polari Book Prize 2020.

'Staggeringly visionary'
– Attitude

'Essential reading'
– Charlie Craggs

'Bold and ground-breaking'
– Owl

'All those layers of expectation that are thrust upon us; boy, masculine, femme, transgender, sexual, woman, real, are such a weight to carry round. I feel transgressive. I feel hybrid. I feel trans.'

In this radical and emotionally raw book, Juno Roche pushes the boundaries of trans representation by redefining 'trans' as an identity with its own power and strength, that goes beyond the gender binary.

Through intimate conversations with leading and influential figures in the trans community, such as Kate Bornstein, Travis Alabanza, Josephine Jones, Glamrou and E-J Scott, this book highlights the diversity of trans identities and experiences with regard to love, bodies, sex, race and class, and urges trans people – and the world at large – to embrace a 'trans' identity as something that offers empowerment and autonomy.

Powerfully written, and with humour and advice throughout, this book is essential reading for anyone interested in the future of gender and how we identify ourselves.

£12.99 | $19.95 | PB | 256PP | ISBN 978 1 78775 019 7 | EISBN 978 1 78775 020 3